CW01507474

CONTENTS

INTRO

Thank you for purchasing my book, and I hope you find the support useful alongside your decision to purchase a static caravan.

Now more than ever, people are looking for an alternative lifestyle, some even to the point of living completely off grid. Having all found ourselves with limited freedom during 2020 and 2021, travelling around or even living in a van quickly became a great alternative, and extremely popular. Not only does it significantly reduce your monthly bills, rent, or mortgage payments, it is also much more fun, and turns every single day into a new adventure.

Speaking for myself, I can honestly say that I came to life when living in a van, and I enjoyed living a life of adventure with my lifestyle no longer being determined by large rental payments. Life always throws curve balls at us, and not all of us will be prepared for some of the challenges which come our way, but the part I love about this, is that with having financial freedom from living an alternative lifestyle, the normal stress and anxiety doesn't happen.

I've lived in different locations around the world, but never in a caravan until my thirties, and I absolutely loved it! It wasn't planned, it actually came about out of desperation and a necessity to put a roof over my head, but I'm a big believer in that everything happens for a reason. Having then got the bug for the freedom it gave me, later down the line I experimented with different types of van life to include static caravans, touring caravans, and converted camper vans.

What I didn't realise, was how living in a caravan suddenly gave me back my freedom, and how it solved every single headache I was having daily, both financially and on a personal level. Over the years I had always struggled with finding affordable property which would allow me to have my dog there, and anyone who knows me knows that my dog was my life. Having an estate agent tell me to give up my dog in order to find a property, would he give up his child, no I doubt it, my dog was part of my family.

As long as my caravan was on a dog friendly park, anything else I could work around. It was seriously like a weight had been lifted, and all of a sudden I had nothing to worry about anymore, and we know we are all guilty of spending hours and days worrying about things we have no control over.

Having moved on from the static caravan and back into bricks and mortar for a while, I wanted to share my story, along with a guide and some tips and advice for those of you considering a holiday caravan purchase or even a move full-time into a caravan or camper. My experience was wholly a positive one, and one I would repeat again in a heartbeat, I have nothing but good memories and smiles just thinking about it.

CHAPTER 1- INITIAL THINGS TO LOOK OUT FOR WHEN PURCHASING

When approaching a static caravan purchase, always ask yourself how much space you feel that you need, and what usage you are using the caravan for, holiday usage, or to reside in it. You will need far more space if planning to live in the van rather than visit it for a few weeks at a time.

Always see if the van already has skirting on it around the base, and if not, see if you can negotiate for this to be included in the price if purchasing a brand new van. The skirting on my first static caravan meant that I already had a large enclosed outside storage area which then obviously gave me the same floor space again. With this being enclosed it meant it was dry, so I decided to store suitcases and outdoor equipment under the van. Make sure the skirting reaches the floor, as this then eliminates the possibility of un-wanted potential visitors being able to squeeze through. I would like to add though that this isn't something that myself or any of my neighbours ever suffered with.

Most sites will also allow you to erect a shed or outside storage unit at the end of your van, so I purchased one of these from Argos and we kept tools and fishing equipment in it. These are questions you will want to ask, as you will normally find that with the larger chains of holiday parks, they will have conditions attached to literally anything that you do on site. It is fairly standard on a large corporate site that you will only be allowed to install a storage unit if purchasing it directly from them, and they will charge astronomical fees such as £500-£700 for a metal shed.

So can you live in a static caravan, the answer is yes, yes you can, and there are plenty in the UK to choose from. There are so many locations and so many vans to choose from, so firstly ask yourself this... who is going to be using it? If the answer is just you, then base your decision on owning it for quite a few years, and choose somewhere you know you can relax. I say this, because it is far from simple to change your mind and sell your van, plus they depreciate in value in the same way that cars do.

Most of the larger chains of holiday parks now offer visitor days when you can have a tour around their site and use their facilities so that you get to try before you buy. Some will even line up some other owners who they know will provide glowing references of their holiday park. Nearly all sites will also have a private owners Facebook page which an owner will have setup for them all to use. I will say however that I've been on some of these pages myself, and that more often than not, the pages are used for moaning about the grass not being cut, or site fees being increased.

I chose Exeter in Devon as a location for my first static caravan, and this was due to the employment opportunities within the area, as well as a local dog care service being on the doorstep. With us both working full-time it was important that my dog wasn't just left alone all day, and his care needed to be part of the decision for choosing a location. I also knew that I had

Exmouth Beach close by, and Cornwall was just over an hour away, so it seemed like the perfect location.

CHAPTER 2 - WHICH CARAVAN, WHICH SITE

This is where you need to do your research and make a list of your requirements.

Firstly, location, and I've discussed this in the previous chapter. Over the years I've met plenty of people who own two caravans and who travel between the two depending on their commitments. This is a fantastic way to live, and something I may consider again in the future, this option gives you so much freedom.

Secondly, what size, caravans start from 28x10ft which is extremely small, and with minimal floor space inside. Do you have children or pets, how many bedrooms do you need, and is the kitchen large enough? Do you need a main family bathroom and an en-suite, and is there room to swing a cat?

Thirdly, budget, can you get the size you need in the location you want, for the funds you have available? Never put yourself in an uncomfortable financial position, remember, site owners will want to sell you the biggest and most expensive van they have, and they will try and tempt you with their finance packages.

You DO NOT need to get yourself into debt to buy a caravan, there are vans for all budgets, and holiday parks and private sites of all sizes. The closer you go to a city, normally the price will go up, the closer you are to a beach, definitely the price will go up, and if you are looking for lots of facilities onsite, then again, increase your budget.

Go to caravan shows, Westpoint at Exeter has a fantastic show most years, and take a look at the location of caravan sales showrooms. I viewed vans in Exeter and in Somerset, and came up with a shortlist of what I needed. If there is a particular van that you want, ask the dealers if they will deliver to a site you have in mind?

Not every holiday park will be prepared to work with you on this one however, if they have surplus stock, they will want you to buy one directly from them, but always speak to them first. If they have an empty plot available, and are guaranteed you are buying there, then tell them what van you want, and more than likely as long as the van will fit onto the plot they have available, they will normally be happy to help. Sites make their money on selling you the vans themselves, so they will want to source and supply the van to you, and over the last few years, fewer sites will now allow you to move your static van to their site. Instead, they will offer to use your current van as a part exchange, or to buy it off you, which leaves you with fewer options.

Some older caravans also only have single glazed windows and electric heating, so ask yourself if being warm all year round is important? It was for me as I really feel the cold, so I knew that double glazing and central heating was a must.

Something important to consider, is this going to be where you spend most of you time, it needs to be comfortable, so going for the cheapest budget caravan won't be comfortable long term. You will find that it has standard fixed furniture which is designed for the holiday market, a tiny under counter fridge, fan heated, and of low quality as a full time home, so cheapest is far from the best.

The first van I owned was small, so with a large dog it was a struggle, but I needed a roof over my head. The fixed corner sofa in the lounge / diner was extremely uncomfortable, and so after a long day at work, it wasn't the easiest place to relax. We would squash together, and try and put our feet up, ensuring that we also gave floor space to the dog.

The van had a very small fridge with tiny freezer section, so we couldn't do the food shops we were used to, and we had to shop every few days and factor this in. Only one person could be in the kitchen at a time, and with it running along one wall, even squeezing past whoever was cooking was extremely difficult.

The bathroom was tiny, and with a shower unit only, you could barely turn around in there when getting out of the shower. It was the norm to knock into the sink and toilet when trying to dry off, and although I can laugh about it now, I found it so frustrating at the time. Barely anywhere to put any products, these were left in baskets and shoved into the corner.

The main bedroom had a standard size double bed, with bedside table either side, and no room to move around, so when climbing into bed on the window side, your bum would rub along the wall, taking the curtains with it and allowing the outside in. Again, I can laugh about it now, but flashing your bum to the world is far from ideal.

When looking at the plot on the site you are considering, does it have a garden, does the van already have decking, if not, is there space for decking? The first van I lived in had a small two tier garden, and room for decking, and it gave me something to start with. Again, ask the site owners before purchasing if they have any restrictions on what you can do with the garden. I had to ask permission to gravel over the grass area, permission to plant flowers etc. and this became frustrating in all honesty as it felt slightly controlling.

When I decided I wanted to have some decking, I had to again ask permission, and was told that I had to use them for this service. They quoted an absolute fortune, and so we decided to build it ourselves, which was tricky. If you don't have permission from the owners to do something to your van or your garden, they can tell you to remove it and return it to the way it was. To them it is a business transaction, and the minute you annoy them, they will always work against you.

We did go ahead and build a decking, and under supervision, and we were made to feel uncomfortable when we did this. Also worth remembering that if you choose to upgrade into a new van on the same site, any money you put into your current van will be lost, and the only person who will profit will be the site owners. This decking was left behind on the van when we upgraded to a larger van, and the owners of the site then dismantled it and built their own decking just to make a point.

Does the potential van come with a parking space, and if so, is it adjacent to the van? There is nothing worse than having a fair walk to your van in the pouring rain with a boot full of shopping. Depending on the lighting around the site at night, it's also far more pleasant to be able to park directly next to your van. If using an overflow car park you then have holidaymakers to consider who will also be using any available parking space, and there is every chance you could come home and find no parking at all.

If you have a second vehicle as we did, find out if there is additional parking available, and more importantly, if there is an additional charge for this. The first year of van ownership there were no additional charges, however, upon returning to the van after the shutdown period in year two, we had a letter advising that going forward there would now be a £50 a month charge for all extra vehicles. Over the year this was an additional £600 to add to the costs, and to be paid monthly to the site.

Going back to asking permission for anything you do, on another site we owned on, we were made to dismantle a metal garden box after the park manager stood by and watched us build it, and said nothing. Once built, he advised us that we had to dismantle it immediately and purchase one from them, completely ridiculous, as they were almost identical.

Choosing the right caravan is so important, and you need to get this right, so make that list, and prioritise in order of what you could compromise on if necessary. To summarise, make sure you consider these points:-

1) Location

2) Size

3) Budget

4) Garden

5) Parking

6) Plot

7) Views

Not necessarily in this order, but use this as a guide to remind yourselves on what may be important for you when making that decision.

Make a shortlist of sites, and arrange some viewings in the location you've chosen. There is never any obligation to buy, and don't ever feel pressured to, especially from a pushy salesman.

CHAPTER 3 - HOW MUCH WILL IT COST

The magic question, how much will it cost...

My first van was £18,000 brand new, and this included the site fees for the rest of the year. I would never have considered this cost if I hadn't been receiving the money from my divorce, along with the affordable monthly payments for the balance. Static caravans can be purchased for as low as £10,000 on a private site, but these will be older, and normally with poor heating systems, no double glazing, and a very worn and out-dated interior.

If you are planning to live in your van all year round then you need to be warm, and the heating system was the top of my list. One of the reasons our van was expensive for the size was due to it having central heating, and double glazing, and very quickly we realised how important this was.

We had to factor in gas bottles for the van, and these were £79 per large bottle which was supplied and delivered on site, so you didn't have to worry about running out or carrying it in your vehicle yourself. This price is variable and the price fluctuates depending on caravan parks and the cost of fuel at the time. We then had an electric meter and were billed electric either monthly or quarterly, which kept it simple.

There was no council tax to pay as it was a holiday park, and no TV license again for the same reason. People who used their vans as a holiday home were already paying for this at their main residence, and those of us who lived there could only stay whilst the park was open, which wasn't all year round, and which I will discuss later on in this book.

Don't forget that you will also need insurance and this is essential for your van, and most sites will insist that you have this, and will want to keep a copy of it on file. I shopped around and obtained insurance for around £180 per year. This covers any flooding for example, but won't cover you for winter issues if you have not prepared your van correctly. Always read through your documents thoroughly.

The annual site fees of this particular park were £2,600 when we first moved there, so divide this into 12 months, and you will see how much cheaper it is than living in a house. Most sites will want this in one lump sum at the beginning of each season, which is normally Feb or March, but remember that you then have nothing further to pay then until the following year.

You may be lucky and find a site which is happy to accept the site fees paid monthly, however this is quite unusual. Sites make their money on sales of the vans, and then on their site fees, so if they have 100 vans on site all paying £2,500 for example, then that's £250,000 coming in within one month for them.

I would like to point out that the fees on this particular site were the cheapest by far of all sites I viewed. The larger parks will charge from £5,000 per annum upwards, and one site was dependant on location of the pitch. If I wanted to be overlooking the sand dunes in Cornwall, the site fees were closer to £8,000 per annum. In order to obtain this pitch they wanted you to also buy one of the more expensive caravans and wouldn't let me purchase a caravan suiting our budget for a beachside pitch. Always make sure that you can pay these site fees, if you don't pay, the park can ask you to leave and that's another issue altogether.

We spent almost a year in the first van before we decided to upgrade into something bigger on the same site. You will find on most sites that people are always selling up for various reasons, and we had already decided that we would never buy brand new again as caravans depreciate so quickly in value. You have to remember that dealers see it as a tin can in a field and that the mark up is huge. A dealer may sell a van to a holiday park for 10k for example, and the park can then sell this on for 20-30k, there is a lot of money to be made in caravans.

Upgrading also doesn't always mean a better van, it may just mean more space, or the addition of double glazing etc. We chose to upgrade into a much larger van, 36x12ft, so wider, and longer, and with a wraparound decking on it with bbq area at the back. This van was much older, and not worth the additional £3,000 in price, however the value to us was the space, and also the increased privacy of where on site it was located. If you want that van, even if it is worth less, there will always be an additional sum involved, and there is no way around this. The site owners can easily sell that other van to another party, and therefore they will see any upgrades as an opportunity to make money again once more, it's just business.

The increase in size also meant a much larger living room, and standalone furniture with a reclining two piece suite, more floor space, an en-suite and a main larger bathroom, larger kitchen, full size fridge freezer, and much more space for the dog. It was larger than some one bedroom flats I've seen, and at last we could stretch out. We purchased a second hand corner sofa which stretched the width of the living room and made it really cosy, and we put pictures up, bought plants, and changed the blinds.

The larger the van, the more scope you have to make it your own, and I decided to remove the two single beds from the twin room, and turn that into a walk in wardrobe and storage area. I decided to remove the dining table and chairs, and instead we built a breakfast bar from a bedroom door, and bought two cheap bar stools I found online.

I thoroughly enjoyed re-designing this van, and always received compliments from other owners on site. You do not need permission to change the interior of your van, but bear in mind that you are altering the value if you choose to sell or upgrade again at a later date.

Also note that we only did this on the older second hand van, and would never start ripping out furniture from a brand new one. If you start removing fixed furniture from a van, you will be weakening the structure. The older van already had freestanding sofas and dining table and chairs, so we were just removing these.

I needed to feel happy to return home after working all day, and finally we felt that we weren't tripping over each other which was a bonus. The decking meant that we could have the door open all summer, and that my dog could walk in and out whenever he felt like it, and we would have the constant stream of fresh air blowing through. We bought some cheap garden furniture, were gifted an old fire pit, and spent most summer evenings at the back on the decking, which was really peaceful.

CHAPTER 4 - DO I HAVE TO BUY

It can be very difficult to rent a caravan if you plan on living in it. Most sites do not rent out vans long term, and most owners don't wish to rent their private vans out to others long term either. On the site I chose, there were a few people renting, but only the very old vans which the site knew they couldn't sell on.

At some of the larger sites you may be able to find an owner with a short term let on offer for three months, but more often than not they won't allow pets, so realistically, buying may be your only option.

If you are looking at residential parks then those will always be for sale, and the prices will rocket. Around my current location in Devon and Cornwall, residential sales seem to be from 150k upwards, and at that price you may as well buy into bricks and mortar. There is a holiday park locally to me now which has bungalow style units which are so old, but extremely expensive, as they give you the access to holiday park living, with a large garden area.

Always have a budget and stick to it, shop around, there are deals to be had, especially in winter when people aren't really looking at caravans. Know the tricks of the trade, if you have seen one advertised on a particular park, then ask to see that one when you get there. Sales staff will want to show you all of the higher priced units, and will even sometimes tell you that the one you want to see has now sold. If you can't afford anything higher in price then tell them straight.

It makes no difference to them if you can afford it not, it is on their land, and your site fees are for the pitch that the unit is on, and they can ask you to remove your unit at any time. If you default on your payments for the unit, the finance company will repossess it just like anything else, and then they will sell it back to the park for even less that it was originally up for sale for. Unless you are prepared to lose your home, do not over commit, and stick to your budget.

Do not buy as an investment, vans do not hold their price, and will only ever be worth trade value back to the park. Do not buy if you think you are going to make a salary out of renting the van out. If the park manage your rentals then you will lose a large part of the income to their fees. They will charge you a commission, and a cleaning cost, and they won't care who they rent your van out to. Look at it another way, why buy a van from a park and pay them for arguments sake, 50k, and then pay them again to have loads of other people also using your van. It may as well be a timeshare with you only buying one week. The park will pack it with bookings, therefore reducing the amount of time you and your family can use it, and you end up paying them for this!

I rented out a second van I purchased on another site, and I would let it out for the summer six weeks which is when I didn't want to use it myself. I used a local cleaner to cover the changeovers, and we managed all bookings ourselves, and we used the money purely to cover the annual site fees. The benefit for us was having a second place to stay, and not having hefty site fees to pay each year as these were now covered.

We were nervous about renting it out, so we restricted who we would allow to use it, no large families, max of one dog etc. We had heard stories of other owners having their vans trashed, and this was the last thing we wanted. We kept the prices high for those six weeks, and always took a deposit, and living nearby we also would drive by once within the first 24 hours of the guests arriving. If we had taken a booking from a couple and then seen that it was a single sex large booking, we would have had no hesitation in throwing them out, and this was made clear in our T's & C's.

This would also stand for no smoking issues, or bringing the BBQ off the patio area onto the plastic decking. As much as this all sounds over the top, we were basing it on the many horror stories we had heard, and we wanted to ensure that we only had respectful guests staying in what was ultimately our second home.

CHAPTER 5 - WINTER IN A CARAVAN

Winters in the UK are harsh, and a caravan is not the best when it comes to insulation. The higher the spec, and the newer the unit, the better the insulation will be, and some units have a full residential spec, so do your research.

Newer units now have double glazing and central heating with radiators just like a house, so there is no reason to be cold at all in the winter. I chose to add larger and additional radiators in the larger second van as I felt that the current ones were too small for some of the room sizes, and this was pretty easy to do. You Tube is a wonderful tool for learning new skills, and we learned so much about caravans, fixing heating systems, installing radiators, and building a breakfast bar.

Most new caravans now have 50mm of insulation in the walls and 80mm insulation in the roof. Skirting around the bottom of the van will ensure the air space below the caravan does not drop as much in temperature, as you obviously lose heat through the roof and the floor. Most caravans come supplied with a Morco Combi boiler and these are easy to maintain, and easy to source spare parts for at a reasonable price.

The boiler is the most expensive item you would have to replace should it go wrong, so worth bearing in mind if purchasing a second hand older caravan. It is good practice to have a gas safety check each year, and the first park insisted on this and wanted to keep a copy of the certificate on file. This was to cover themselves in case of any fires etc. and to show that owners were being responsible. The cost of the annual check will normally be between £80-100 per year, and when phoning around gas safety engineers, make sure you always tell them that the boiler is in a caravan. The Gas safety engineer should be qualified for working on caravans, yes it is gas, but it is butane gas instead of natural gas, which is what you would normally find in a domestic house. These are different, as caravans run on what is known by LPG (Low Pressure Gas).

During any shutdown period you MUST prepare your van for the winter. This is to ensure that your pipes don't freeze, there is no fire risk, and that your van remains in good condition. If you have not drained down your static caravan correctly, you may not be covered on insurance during the winter, and could have a claim for damage refused.

The park your van is sited on will normally offer a drain down winter service to you at an additional cost, but it is fairly easy to do this yourself. Make sure you purchase antifreeze, and dehumidifiers, or grab some bowls and fill with salt.

Just follow the easy guide below to ensure you cover everything : -

1) Flush all toilets until the cisterns are empty, and using antifreeze, use the correct measure to pour into the toilet pans, and into any u-bends, including the kitchen sink.

2) Turn any tap on inside, and shut the water off from the main stop cock outside. This will usually be located underneath or next to the van. You will know that the water is off as there

will be nothing running through the tap inside which you've already left on.

3) Turn off any gas supply, and if using gas bottles, make sure you disconnect any bottles from the van (make sure you've turned off the gas first).

4) Disconnect the shower hoses, and turn the showers on, again, no water should be coming through if you have turned off the water correctly.

5) Set up dehumidifiers or a bowl of salt in every room

6) Move any soft furnishings away from the walls in case of damp, leave bedroom doors open to help air flow, and clean all surfaces, empty bins and fridge etc.

This is what we did every winter, and we never had any issues at all. We do know owners that choose to leave their heating on throughout the winter, and this comes down to personal choice.

Some owners also remove curtains and take them home to wash ready for the new season, and some stand their mattress upright.

DO NOT LEAVE ANY VALUABLES IN YOUR VAN DURING CLOSURE, you will not have access to your van, and most sites will not have onsite security.

CHAPTER 6 - HOW LONG CAN MY VAN STAY THERE

Every park will provide you with a contract, and it will state how long your unit can remain on their site for. Make sure that you check this, and don't be caught out if purchasing an older van which no longer fits in with the look of the park. It may be that within a few years you will be asked to remove your van and purchase a new one. If you choose not to purchase new from the park, you may be liable for the costs of removing your old unit, otherwise you will just have to walk away from it and let the park have it back.

When choosing your park, also ask how many months of the year they are open for, another key question. If they are only open for 9 months of the year, and you are planning to live in your unit, what do you plan to do when the park is closed?

The first park I purchased at was only open for ten months of the year, and every January and February they would close which meant we needed somewhere else to go. The first year, and due to finances, it meant a touring caravan, and I discuss this in the next chapter. Year two we had some friends offer us their annex for the two months which was perfect. I was starting a new contract and could do without worrying about accommodation, so this was perfect timing. They were a lovely family, and their children absolutely loved having my dog around the house, although their cat didn't seem as keen.

Year three we managed to find another caravan on another holiday park which we could rent for the two months. This worked perfectly as it was only up the road, and it meant we had full use of the facilities whilst on site, gym, spa, restaurant, and this actually felt like being on another holiday.

If you are planning therefore to live in your van, make sure you confirm if the park will be closed for any months of the year, and don't leave this until the last minute to figure out where you will go for any closure periods.

You may be lucky and find a 12 month holiday park who will turn a blind eye to you living there, I actually currently know of one on the outskirts of Exeter, but good things don't last forever. The bottom line is that you should not be living there, and the local council who issued the license to the holiday park can check owners details at any time. They have a right to ask who owns the caravans on site, and therefore can check if those concerned are paying council tax or are registered at another address. On the flip side of this though, one site owner advised me that if the Council then threw everyone off site, they would need to house all of those people. I have heard of sites receiving hefty fines for allowing residents, so this is something you need to be aware of.

Remember what I mentioned previously, you could always have a second van in another location, and therefore you aren't actually living full-time in either. You could also have one static van on one site, and a touring caravan on a seasonal pitch at another site, or a static and a camper van. You could also travel, or stay with friends occasionally in order to show that you are away from your van. All is not lost, you just need to understand the rules, and think outside the box.

CHAPTER 7 - HOW LONG IS THE SEASON

Year one and with barely anything to my name, the first site owner had offered me details of a contact he knew who rented out touring caravans, and would deliver them to site for you to use during the 2 month closure. The park owner would then allow you to rent one of his touring pitches for the two months which remained open. With this particular site, the static caravans were for ten months of holiday use, however his touring caravan park remained open for twelve months. Again, every site will be different, and most parks will close the whole site, not just part of it.

This meant we could stay in the same location, but had to move out of our static home, and stay within 5 metres, but in a touring caravan. However, this was the only option for the first year, and at an additional cost of £500 per month for the two months, I viewed and then chose one of only two pet friendly touring caravans on offer.

This was the only negative memory I have of caravan living, two large adults and one very large dog, all in a tiny 2 berth caravan for 2 months, and during the winter months. By this point I had no further work once my contract came to an end, and therefore would be spending all day in this touring caravan, something I wasn't looking forward to. When I say it was small, you literally had to go outside to change your mind.

Being that I like to take a positive from every bad situation however, we were still able to cook a full Sunday roast in the touring caravan, and it did provide a lot of laughter, eventually...

I remember the touring caravan being dropped off and us starting to pack to move into it, and we could barely fit anything in. Night one and we decided to grab a takeaway to soften the blow, but the lights went out as we started to tuck in. We sat there with one candle eating our takeaway while huddling together with the dog, and I decided at this point that I would never be in this position again. The TV wouldn't tune in, the electrics had completely gone off, and in the dark there was nothing we could do about it that evening.

You then had the weather and movement of the van which came as quite a shock on the first night. With high winds and rain we barely slept, and it was like having a free cruise as the van rocked all over the place. The dog became anxious and restless, and it was far from my idea of fun. It was a horrendous first night, and one I will never forget.

Back into the static caravan in March for the rest of the season, and it was great catching up with the other owners and finding out where everyone had been for the shutdown period. You would see other new owners repeating the pattern of renting a touring caravan for the first winter shutdown just as we had. Speaking to them when returning in March was always interesting, and more often than not they vowed to never do it again, just as we did. Don't get me wrong, some people had their own touring caravans in storage that were huge and luxurious, and they didn't mind at all staying in these for two months, but these people were few and far between.

There are plenty of winter rentals out there, and it became quite an adventure the following year to be able to move to a larger and much more luxurious holiday park for those two months. It actually felt like we were on holiday, and with the view of a fishing lake, and wrap around decking, we actually really enjoyed it. With so many facilities on site, and in a beautiful woodland location, this was by far the best experience of the winter shutdown over the three years of owning that static caravan.

CHAPTER 8 - ON SITE COMMUNITY

Very quickly you will meet other owners and depending on where you are and how large the site is, you can find yourself part of a friendly owner's community. If you own on a large holiday park then the owners will normally have events and trips arranged.

If this is something you are looking for, then again add it to you wish list, and even ask to speak to other owners. Most large sites will have an owners Facebook page which someone will have set up, and this is a great source of information for you.

The first park I owned on didn't have this, and although everyone was friendly and would stop and talk, nobody socialised together at all, or seemed interested to. This was absolutely fine back then, but now I would prefer to have a social side to living on a holiday park.

If you are buying as a holiday home on one of the larger holiday parks, they will also have exclusive owner events arranged, and it is more likely that you will find plenty of owners socialising who all head to their holiday homes for the summer months. Don't think that only the older generation will be buying these units, I was in my 30's when I first purchased, and the other owners were all different ages and backgrounds.

I loved listening to peoples stories of how they got there, and why. On the smaller park it was made up of people returning from living abroad, people who had lost their jobs, people getting divorced, people developing and renovating property, all walks of life. On the first park there was a driving instructor, a chef, a Formula one team member, teachers, tradesmen, it was such an interesting group of people.

Nobody was ashamed of living in caravans, and everyone embraced it, and people came and went quickly. The three years we lived there we saw so many people sell up, those who didn't enjoy the lifestyle, those who could now afford a house, relationship breakdowns, new jobs, relocating to other areas, we met so many interesting people.

The only downside to this was if you wanted to really keep yourself to yourself, it was impossible to walk the dog around the park and not bang into anyone. It was impossible to use the laundry rooms on weekends and not see anyone while in there. You had to walk past other units to get to wherever you were going, so this is another thing to bear in mind.

If you want to feel like you are on holiday every day though, and make new friends, have facilities on your doorstep, then this may be the life for you. There is even a regular TV programme about Brits who have purchased caravans over in Spain and are enjoying being part of a fab community. If you watch these programmes, you will see that caravan sites in Spain, Italy, France and even Greece for example will have a large social scene, with owners all being on first name terms.

There is a company called Caravans in the Sun who advertise sales in other countries fairly regularly, and who attend trade shows, as well as all the FB groups and pages you can find, so you really do have so many options. Depending on your budget, you can quite easily pick two vans up for between 50-60k total for the two. Again though, don't compromise on your requirements if you need central heating, double glazing, and a certain amount of space.

CHAPTER 9 - IS CARAVAN LIFE ENJOYABLE

This depends on the reasons you are purchasing in the first place, and what you are expecting to get out of it.

A caravan was not my first choice, but once I had settled into it, I enjoyed every single minute. I had freedom, no large rental payments or mortgage around my neck, and even when I was out of work, I didn't have to panic about rent and large bills to pay.

Having no money worries at all improved my mental health from the get go, and I knew every single month what we needed to put aside for the site fees the following year. We knew how many gas bottles we would use a year, how much electric we would use, and there were no surprise bills coming in.

We had the most amazing views of the countryside, and we would sit around our fire pit on the back of the decking and watch the sunset across the fields. We were relaxed, my dog was relaxed, and there was nothing to worry about. We owned our own home, and nobody could ever take it away from us, so we no longer needed to worry about our security.

The holiday makers who stayed on the touring pitches were

always happy due to being on holiday, and they would come and go throughout the summer, sad to be leaving to head home. We would sit there and reflect on how lucky we were to be living there without needing to leave.

Occasionally a holiday maker would fall in love with the lifestyle enough to use their touring caravan as a part exchange against a static caravan, and to then also start their new life.

I can honestly say that during those three years, we never met any owner who regretted purchasing their unit, not once! Some may regret the site they purchased on, and this would always come down to the site rules that they didn't agree with, but nobody ever regretted the lifestyle itself, and that tells me everything.

I never look back at those years as a negative, and I've only taken positive experiences away from those years. I would return to that lifestyle again if I needed to, and I already have my list of holiday parks ready for when that time comes.

Since the pandemic however, prices of caravans to buy have increased ridiculously, with static caravans previously offered at 30k, now being as high as 50-60k for the same van. With people being prepared to pay these prices, they will never drop back down, so currently I have no intention of purchasing another static van in the future, and with a camper van and a touring van on a seasonal pitch, the urgency is no longer there.

Don't put your dreams on hold though if this is what you want. I know people who have paid 80k for a caravan, an older couple who have sold their home and paid 150k for a lodge, if you have the money, and you want to switch up your lifestyle for an alternative way of living, then go for it!

CHAPTER 10 - CAN I MOVE MY VAN

You may think this is a strange question, but stay with me on this one.

When you decide you want to leave the caravan / holiday park, what are you planning on doing with your unit? Have you even thought this far ahead, and if not, then make sure you do. Yes, we can all live in the present moment, but this is important if you think you may not stay long term where you are planning to purchase.

The park itself may or may not be interested in buying your unit back from you, and if they are, it will be at a rock bottom price. They will rarely ever negotiate, and the minute you sign that deal to sell, they will inflate the price right up again and sell it to the next person. There is no point in getting angry about this, it's business, not personal, and the way it works in so many industries, buy low, sell high.

You will have the option of selling your unit privately, but most parks will have written into your contract that they have the final say on who buys it. They can make it very difficult for new people to buy, as obviously they would prefer the prospective new owners to buy directly from them. They may use underhand tactics such as telling new buyers that your van has heating issues or leaks, anything to put them off, this is known as sale blocking, however trying to prove it will always be difficult as nobody ever wants to speak up.

You then have the commission they charge for overseeing the deal, and this is normally around 15%. This is fairly standard, and you are not able to get around this, most parks will even make you do the deal in their office so they can see how much the new owner is paying for your van. We've seen it all, owners who ask their buyers to lie about the price in order to reduce the commission they will owe. The park owners find out, put a stop to the sale, and can throw the current owners off site. Lying about your sale price or anything else just isn't worth the stress if the site owners find out.

Always remember that your unit is on their land, and they will always have the final say. You cannot out smart them, they have seen it all before, and they know the tricks. Just be mindful that if you are selling privately in order to get a high price, that you will be liable to pay more commission to the park.

You then have the option of removing your van and taking it elsewhere, much easier said than done. Where exactly do you think you will be taking it, most parks will not allow you to bring your own van to their site, so that leaves you with minimal options of where to take it. There isn't enough money for a new park to make if you aren't buying from them. A few parks may offer a gate fee for you to bring your own van, and they can name their price, so you need to decide how important it is for you to keep the same van, and if it is worth the stress.

A further option is to sell it to a dealer and let them arrange collection and removal. It will cause tension with the current park, but will normally return you a higher price, you just have to stand your ground. I did this with my last van, and as soon as I had arranged collection and a sale through a dealer, the park owners then matched the offer in order for me not to remove it.

They then bumped the price back up and re-sold the van again.

It just seems like one big game, everyone trying to get the best deal, and it can be very stressful, those few weeks weren't fun at all. We had a new van on another site ready to move into, and meanwhile we were having to jump through hoops and play games with the old van. If you just want shot of your old unit, then sell it back to the park and walk away. Keep in mind though that if your unit is old and run down, more often than not the park will offer you nothing and tell you that they don't want it at all. This can be another sales tactic though, once you walk away from it, they still re sell it on, they've had it back for free, and it starts all over again.

CHAPTER 11 - ISSUES & SOLUTIONS

1) Where Do I Send My Mail?

You can't receive mail to a holiday park, and this is normal and has been the same at all parks I've lived on, and is fairly standard, especially if it is not a residential park.

Solution

I was able however to rent a mailbox on an industrial estate near the first park, and all post and parcels were sent there. It did mean that I had to go and collect it as often as possible, and I had a cost of approximately £20 per month to pay for this, but this was still the easiest way to get access to any post. The other option is to have mail sent to a friend or family member nearby for you to collect. It doesn't have to be an issue though, and you shouldn't see it as one, considering most post to a home address is a bill, and you won't be receiving loads of these anymore.

2) Car Insurance

You also can't insure your car to a holiday park address. The car is on private property, and is completely safe at the park, but insurance companies won't allow you to insure there if you aren't registered as living there. Only members of staff at the

Park are able to do this.

Solution

Most people I met living on holiday parks insure their car to a nearby friend's house or family member, extremely near by. If you aren't honest with your car insurance company though, they have the right to invalidate your insurance.

3) Downsizing

You can't erect extra buildings or storage next to your van, so will be downsizing from your current home into a property the size of a flat.

Solution

Rent a storage unit nearby for those items you don't need every day, but don't want to get rid of. You can even keep valuables at the storage unit until you get to know the site you are on and until you feel comfortable with leaving your van empty.

CHAPTER 12 - SUMMARY

Caravan life is a great life, affordable for all types of budget even if you have low paid work or other financial commitments. Apart from the initial purchase of a static caravan or lodge, overall running costs are considerably cheaper than living in a residential house.

No one can take away from you what is yours, no risk of being evicted by a landlord because they wish to resell their property or decide that a family member needs to move into their property. No issues with having a pet, or noisy neighbours, or messy neighbouring gardens either. Just remember to know the park rules and abide by them so as not to make the owner/staff unhappy, and always pay what is owed to ensure a calm, stress free life.

Refer to this guide if you are in any doubt of what to look for, and remember that your gut feeling is normally right. Visit the park, holiday at the park, and speak to other owners if possible. Join the owners FB park pages and ask for opinions on that park. Do your research, and if you don't like the park owners when you meet them, or they aren't willing to answer your questions, then this isn't the park for you. Once you make your decision, it won't be easy if you change your mind, and you will never get back the price you paid for your unit.

Factor in the extra costs of insurance, winter shutdown rental elsewhere, gas bottles, electric, car parking, annual site fees, and make sure those costs are affordable and comfortable for you.

Are you planning on sub-letting your unit on one of the larger parks, and if so, does the site allow it? If you are planning on sub-letting, does the park allow you to do this yourself or does it have to go through them? Unless renting your unit out to cover those annual site fees, there really isn't any point.

Do you see yourself wanting a unit at that park for 5-10 years? If something goes wrong, and you want to leave / sell up, are you happy with losing so much money on the price of your unit, and will that then put you in a difficult financial position?

CHAPTER 13 - SEASONAL PITCH OPTIONS

Fast forward to now, and I currently own a touring caravan which I have placed on a seasonal pitch in Cornwall. Initially I placed it on a pitch in Devon due to needing to be close to a family member suffering with an illness. Great family run site, but with no facilities at all, and by far the most expensive touring site I had ever come across.

Chosen purely for the location, and grateful that I wasn't tied into a contract, I was able to give notice and move the caravan without any trouble at all. I knew I wanted to move it closer to home, so I could keep an eye on it, but also escape the peak season madness and get some use out of it myself.

I found the caravan online after spending months looking for one, and I managed to get a great deal from a private seller who was desperate to sell. On the day of delivery, the owner at the time blew the electrics by using a cheap generator, and I wasn't impressed. This situation did however enable me to get a further chunky lump sum off the asking price, and having googled the cost of a new electric unit, I knew it wasn't going to be an issue to rectify.

I looked at several pitches in Cornwall, and had my eye on one in particular, however their opening day kept being pushed back, and I had to remove the van from the site in Devon by a particular date, so in the end, I opted for a site which was actually closer to home and that I hadn't previously given much thought to. Everything happens for a reason though, and this site has a longer season, is almost a third cheaper, and is beautiful.

The pitch is huge, there's so much space, and the shower blocks are well looked after. The grounds are beautiful, and there is so much space for dog walking, barbecuing, and relaxing of course. We've removed and resealed the rear skylight after noticing a small leak, but this is now rectified, and hasn't done any long term damage. I plan to re-decorate the inside, as it's quite an old van, and I would like to make it more modern and brighter, so this is on my list.

I now feel like I have that little slice of heaven to retreat to when the town centre gets too busy, and also it gives me a little project. With house prices the way they are, and landlords increasing rents across the board, it also provides me with some security if anything were to happen with my current property.

CHAPTER 14 - CAMPER VAN OPTION

Ever thought about converting an empty van so you can drive around and visit different locations rather than staying in one place? We have ourselves converted three vans, the first was a Mercedes Vito, the second was a Fiat Ducato, and the third was an LDV Maxus. We had no experience of van conversions, and we researched and watched videos for hours and hours. With our passion for vanlife in general, when the opportunity came up with a cheap shell of a van, we jumped at it.

The Mercedes Vito wasn't a full conversion, we just wanted it carpeted and with a bed in it so that we could have weekends away, and with enough room for our dog. We didn't want to rush into a purchase, we had a limited budget, so we waited until Christmas week when we knew people would be trying to raise some last minute funds, and we ended up with having a few to choose from.

We drove to Cardiff to view a green Vito which looked great in the Ebay photos, however close up it was a mess. Even though the price was right, we knew we would have a lot of work to put in, and probably a few issues with it further down the line. Whilst in Cardiff another one was posted on Ebay, and again at the right price, and this looked spotless, but it was in London. Following a quick discussion and our craving for adventures, we set off, stopping to grab some lunch at the services along the way, and a quick dog walk.

We found the address in Hendon fairly quickly, and the van was immaculate and just what we were looking for. Having negotiated a steal of a price, we laid down the money, and set off back home with the van. Stopping off again on the way home to let the dog out and grab some dinner, it was a long day, and we were glad to reach home.

The following day we inspected the van for any issues which needing working on such as welding, we cleaned the van up, and made a plan of action for what we needed to do. We decided to remove the rear seven seats to give us the whole back area for the bed, and we realised that the rear seats would fetch a good price. We sold them all individually and made just over £450 for the seats which went back into the pot for the refurb.

We purchased sound deadening and insulation bubble wrap, and then purchased a carpet to lay on top. This already brought so much warmth to the van, and was literally all we needed to do. The windows already had curtains, and the van had a drop down small TV screen at the front, so we were good to go.

The first trip way we just stuck a mattress and bedding in the back and took off to Devon with the dog. Staying on campsites it all worked perfectly, using their facilities, eating out every night, and only having the nightly cost of the campsite. We removed the mattress and added a click clack sofa bed which we picked up cheaply, however this was the most uncomfortable bed we ever stayed on, so we only used it once, and left it in the van when we sold it.

We had the bug, and with winter coming and some welding work needing doing, we sold the Vito and made almost double to what we had paid for it. We already knew we wanted to take on another van, but decided to wait until we had settled elsewhere as we were also looking at moving house and were both facing redundancy.

Several years passed before we had time to start looking at another project, and this time we decided on a Fiat Ducato for the space it would give us. We spotted one in Torquay which was gold, and off we went to view it. I didn't like the colour at all, but I knew it was a good deal, so we negotiated hard and left with the van.

This van had transported diesel at some point in the back and it smelt so strongly, so that became the first part of the project. With the rear being empty, we just jet washed it thoroughly a few times and left the doors open to air it out which seemed to work. We removed the bulkhead to make the whole space open in the van, and we started to plan the layout of everything we wanted to include.

This van was a bigger project as we were including a seated area, a full size double bed, wall mounted TV, and kitchen area. We put sound deadening on all walls and floor area, and ply lined the back. We decided we wanted vinyl rather than carpet as flooring this time, so purchased some vinyl from Ebay and then got that laid.

CONCLUSION

Hopefully you have found this guide useful and supportive with making a decision which is right for you. Whether it be a static caravan, a tourer, or even a converted camper, you can make every day an adventure, and thousands of people are now doing this both for financial and lifestyle reasons. You can live in any of these very comfortably and make it your own, have fab neighbours, and make some amazing friends. For me personally I will be looking at this to see my years out rather than some ridiculously expensive rental property in the UK.

Would I live in a static caravan again, absolutely, but I wouldn't ever purchase one just to use occasionally, or on the basis of needing to rent it out for the majority of the year, definitely not. If this is the case for you, it will be much cheaper to just rent one each time you want a holiday, and have the flexibility of different sites each time.

Don't get shiny object syndrome and over stretch yourself, buying the largest and most luxurious. Keep in mind that a caravan is a tin can in a field, it is the interior which is different. If you aren't keeping the van long term, then remember that you will only be offered trade value back from the park when you want to sell your van and move on.

I have met some amazing people during my caravan years, and I love how simple they all made their lives. Some owning in two locations, some owning abroad and travelling between the two, feeling like they are on a never ending holiday, bliss! Another benefit of doing this is that they can rent one of them out for the summer six weeks as mentioned in a previous chapter, and this will cover those second site fees. Do make sure that the site will allow this though, as my first site wouldn't allow sub-letting, and this was written into the contract.

One of my friends still owns a static caravan in Cornwall, and they use theirs every single month for minimum of a week. It works absolutely perfectly for them, and for their children and grandchildren, and they have a gorgeous residential large lodge style caravan with one of the most beautiful interiors I have ever seen. This came at a price though of just under 100k, and personally I would never spend this on a caravan.

I believe that life is meant to be lived, and is meant to be an adventure, if we were meant to stay in one place, we would have roots. You are not a tree, so move around, enjoy yourself, and make the most of every day you have. Whether it be a static caravan, or a converted day van, let van life set you free.

A freedom lifestyle to go wherever I want, whenever I want, yes please.

ABOUT THE AUTHOR

I'm Natalia, now in my 40's, and now living full time down in Cornwall. My background is within the corporate world in London, which is where I spent many years of my life in the rat race. During those years my driving force was salary and material things, and looking back now, I realise that at no point did those things make me happy. All I ever wanted was freedom, freedom to come and go as I like, and not have a person or company controlling my working hours, my holiday allowance, and even dictating when I could and couldn't holiday, telling me that I needed to fit in with other people.

I've owned a total of three static caravans, one tourer, and three camper vans over the years, and have viewed well over one hundred static vans across different parks and different locations within the South West of the UK. I have written this book based on my own personal experience of caravan ownership, and hope that it can help others looking to purchase.

Thank you for reading, and it would be appreciated if you could provide a short review on Amazon in order to raise awareness of this guide.

With gratitude

Natalia

Printed in Great Britain
by Amazon

40399126R00030